Dear Scott,

Every Day Is Christmas

imagine what it would be like
to bring in a bit of Xmas Spirit
every day of the year (along with
some blue energy!) ?!?!

Have an inspirational 2008!

Missak

Other Books by Bradley Trevor Greive

The Blue Day Book*

The Blue Day Journal and Directory

Dear Mum*

Looking for Mr Right

The Meaning of Life

The Incredible Truth About Mothers

Tomorrow

Priceless: The Vanishing Beauty of a Fragile Planet

The Book for People Who Do Too Much

Friends to the End*

Dear Dad

The Simple Truth About Love

A Teaspoon of Courage

Dieting Causes Brain Damage

For Children

The Blue Day Book for Kids

Friends to the End for Kids

*Available in Spanish

Every Day Is Christmas

BRADLEY TREVOR GREIVE

**Andrews McMeel
Publishing, LLC**

Kansas City

Attention: Schools and Businesses
Andrews McMeel books are available at quantity discounts with bulk purchase for educational,
business, or sales promotional use. For information, please write to: Special Sales Department,
Andrews McMeel Publishing, LLC, 4520 Main Street, Kansas City, Missouri 64111.

Photo Credits
ALAMY/ TRI-SCAN (Australia) www.photosforme.com
AMANDA JONES (USA) www.amandajones.com
AUSCAPE (Australia) www.auscape.com.au
AUSTRAL (Australia) www.australphoto.com.au
CORBIS AUSTRALIA PTY LTD www.corbis.com
DANIEL J. COX / NATURAL EXPOSURES (USA) www.naturalexposures.com
GETTY IMAGES www.gettyimages.com
JUPITER IMAGES (Australia) www.jupiterimages.com.au
NATURE PICTURE LIBRARY (UK) www.naturepl.com
PHOTOLIBRARY (Australia) www.photolibrary.com
PREMIUM (Germany) www.premiumnatur.de
WILDLIGHT PHOTO AGENCY (Australia) www.wildlight.net

Detailed page credits for the remarkable photographers whose work appears in *Every Day Is Christmas*
and other books by Bradley Trevor Greive are freely available at www.btgstudios.com.

Acknowledgments

Ever since I was a little boy with a shiny face and a fistful of ill-gotten confectionary, I have looked forward to our family Christmas. Each year my mother would rally my sisters and me to decorate the tree, though I must confess my sisters did almost all the work whilst I would lie on the floor playing with the beautiful ornaments and figurines. My favourites were the Indian reindeers that had little mirrored pieces stitched to their glossy flanks. My father would sit on the sofa and make abstract observations that were no help to anyone who could be bothered to listen, and later one of the family pets would attack the tree and we would start all over again.

I have never missed a family Christmas gathering in my life, and I plan never to let that happen. Not that I was always home on December 25. During my years in the army and, more recently, with various international obligations, sometimes I was absent on this special day. But my family would always make the time for a special Christmas celebration together whether it was a week late or a month early—and I loved that.

In fact, it was our flexible family Christmas dates that first gave me the idea for this little book. In a rare moment of clarity I thought, hey, if *any day could be Christmas* then why can't *every day be Christmas*? The more I read about the history of the world's most important holiday, the more it made sense. We can and should celebrate the joys and values of Christmas with those we love far more often than once a year.

When you mention the word "Christmas", most selfish people immediately think of receiving gifts—I know I do. And some of the gifts I am most grateful for are the people who make my life as enjoyable as it is. I am so thankful for my wise, long-suffering editor in Kansas City, Christine Schillig, and also Nerida Robinson, who fearlessly leads my team at BTG STUDIOS in Australia. I am also grateful to Mrs Jacqueline Barr who, like a happy Christmas elf, always jumps in to help me get things done in Tasmania. I would be lost without these wonderful people.

Clearly this book would not be what it is without the many extraordinary photographers and image libraries throughout the world with whom I collaborate. I encourage everyone interested in superb professional photography to seek out their updated contact details posted at www.btgstudios.com.

Of course, in my world, the benevolent and jolly ambassador of Christmas is not a chubby old fellow with a white beard but a buff Jewish gentleman with a glittering silver moustache—my long-time literary agent and dear friend, Albert J Zuckerman of Writers House, New York.

I remember one cold December morning in Manhattan when we waded through several feet of snow and slush towards an uptown tennis club where I would endure the Christmas tradition of straight sets lost. As we passed the Christmas tree sellers dusting off their stock for early commuters, Al stopped to admire a voluptuous fir and said, "Bradley, my boy, don't you think it curious that we take these beautiful trees into our homes only after they are already dying?" I had never considered this rather morbid thought before, and so I just looked blank and shivered in my tracksuit. "My point is", he continued, "everything that is alive and beautiful about Christmas, Hanukkah, Kwanzaa, whatever, is in our hearts and homes already. The beautiful thing is that, for a time at least, we give this tree new life with the love in our hearts, just as we give life to everything that is beautiful in our world by sharing that love in our hearts."

With that, Al turned to the Christmas tree seller, paid for the best tree she had, and then stopped her from actually giving it to him. He simply put his hand on her arm gently and said, "Next year, cut down one less tree for me, okay?" We all shared a quiet smile, and then we went on our way.

Thank you, Sir Albert, for showing me the beauty of Christmas.

Every Day Is
Christmas

The wait is over!

At last, the Christmas spirit has completed the
twelve-month journey back to our hearts.

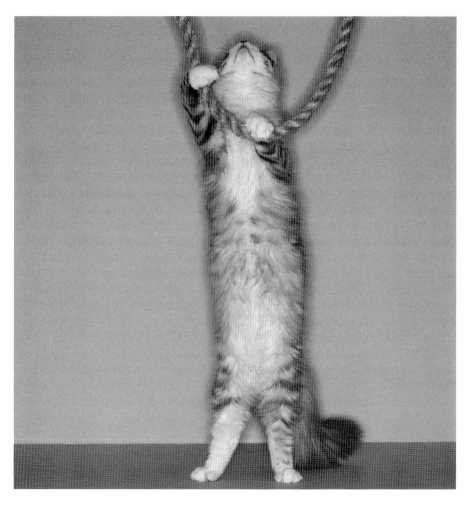

Listen as the midnight air is split crisply and sweetly by the
heavy tolling of large, ponderous church bells.

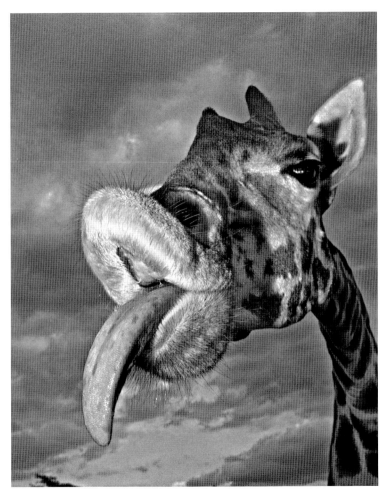

Taste the sugared wonders and delights that send even the
most wooden tongues into quivering ecstasy.

Gaze upon the glittering bloom of decorations that transform
our streets and homes into a garden of stars.

For many, great feasting is the highlight, leaving them in a
state of trouser-rending immobility, waistlines polished and straining
like sacks of Christmas pudding adrift at sea.

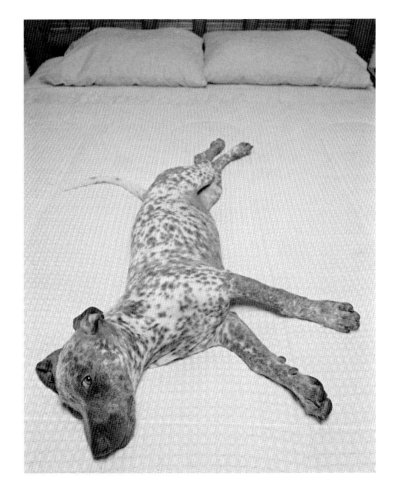

As homes fill with gifts, the nights drag on interminably for those who struggle to contain the festive frenzy fizzing within, tossing and turning, hoping their transgressions might be overlooked just this once.

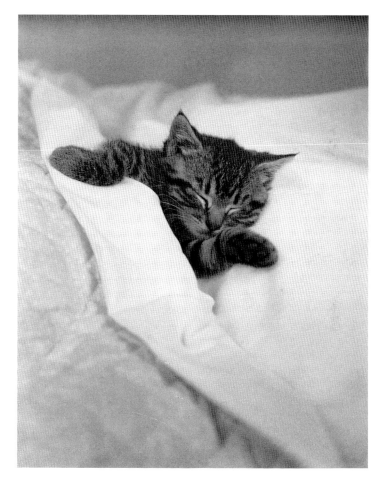

Meanwhile, a select few "enjoy the honey-heavy dew of slumber" that only a genuinely clear conscience or premium legal representation can provide.

But no matter how much intoxicating seasonal excitement,
earnest yammering, radiant fluffery, and plastic decoration we indulge in,
these things do not explain the fundamental enduring joy of Christmas
or answer the one truly interesting question:

What does Christmas really mean today?

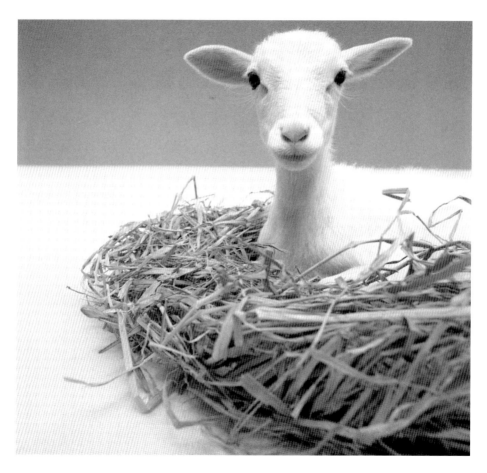

The answer, of course, can be found in the straw of the fabled Bethlehem stable some 2000 years ago. The birth of Jesus Christ was, in every meaningful way, the birth of hope. To this day, Christmas remains a joyful celebration of hope reborn for both Christians and non-Christians alike.

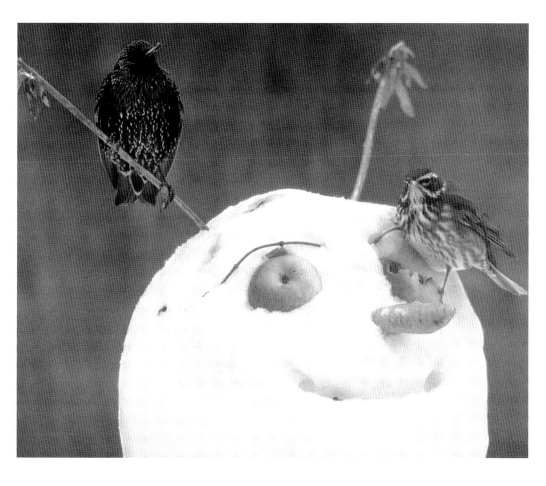

The way this manifests itself varies greatly from place to place and culture to culture. While people in Europe and North America might enjoy Christmas Eve amid legions of mitten-moulded snowmen,

at exactly the same time, many Australians and Africans
will celebrate while making sand angels at the beach.

Regardless of the many different interpretations and religious beliefs,
the simple, universal truth about the holiday season
is that billions of people, from all walks of life, look forward to
this time of year in a state of joyous wonderment.

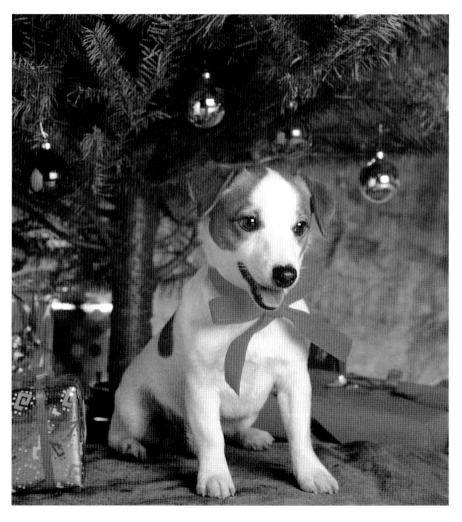

After all, it is a truly magical time.

So magical that even folks who have been fixated on their own lot
now invest serious time thinking about what they can do
to brighten up someone else's life—a compete reversal
of the often maligned human condition.

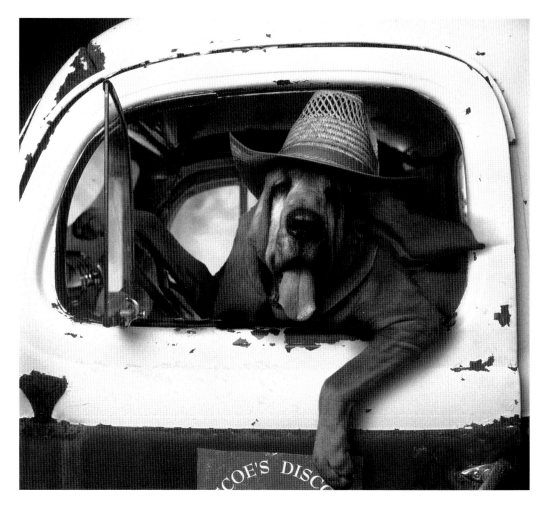

And as if that weren't enough, cabbies and lorry-drivers are suddenly polite and friendly, even in Newcastle on a Saturday night!

There are so many wonderful things to enjoy on the world's greatest holiday. For starters, Christmas *is* a holiday and for many of us that means a long-overdue rest.

As the spirit revives, we have a chance to
uncork the champagne and celebrate life, love, and laughter
in whatever ratio feels right, and legal, at the time.

Who can forget the joy of finding the perfect gift
for someone you adore?

Christmas means traditional carols and a host of holiday favourites
that bring back wonderful memories and make you want to sing out loud—
even when you know you shouldn't.

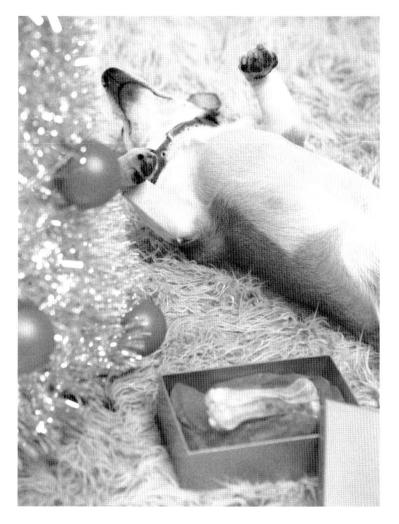

It means being drunk with joy and perhaps a little eggnog to boot.

It means an abundance of sincere *thank you*'s and *you're welcome*'s.

And as it has for more than a thousand years,
Christmas means togetherness.

Christmas is the best day of the year to observe and uphold the
true value of family. It reforges the lifelong bond between family members
and reminds them just how much they have in common,
regardless of where life has taken them.

"Hey, wait a minute. If *I* brought the brandy,
and *you* brought the brandy—then *who* brought the food?"

Of course, we can't forget the exchange of presents, which—like kissing—
is an extremely gratifying exercise for all parties but also involves
the exquisite agony of anticipation that makes it difficult
for people to hide their excitement.

Normally reserved folks resort to the "Christmas creep", sneaking quietly around the house at all hours to peek at the gifts piling up beneath the Christmas tree to see which ones are theirs.

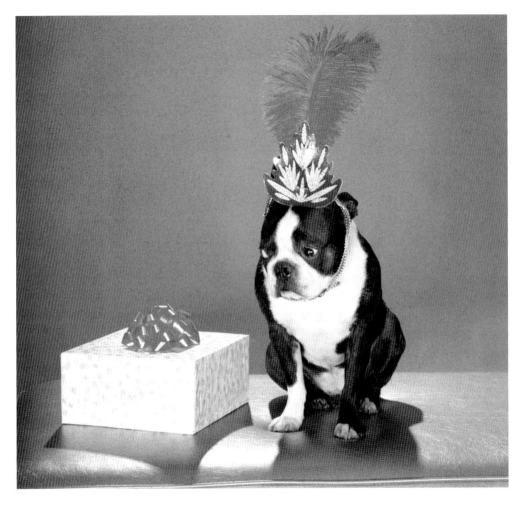

Watching people try to guess what is inside each gift-wrapped parcel
seems to disprove the existence of ESP.

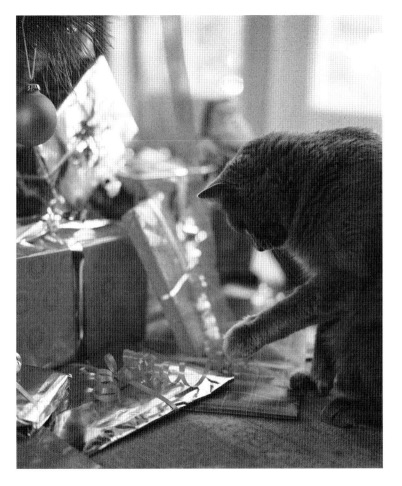

Still, the act of gently shaking and jostling presents to
ascertain their contents can be wickedly exciting,
pleasantly confounding, and, just occasionally, enlightening.

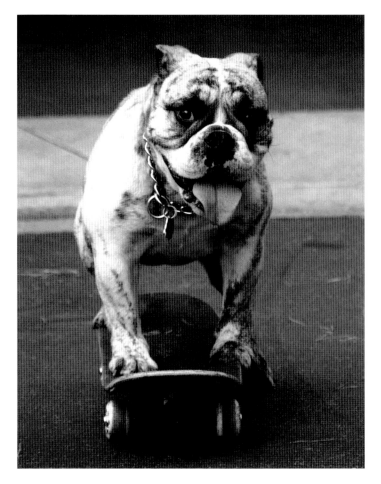

At last the moment of revelation arrives, and there you are, enraptured
to the point of rupture, face to face with that one special thing that you have
yearned for every waking moment since last Christmas . . .

unless what you really wanted was a first edition of *Ulysses* by James Joyce, and maybe some nice body lotion with jojoba.

With everyone watching (and they are *all* watching), you now have
to endure the seemingly endless and undignified horror of gallantly
pretending that your gift was just what you were dreaming of.

There are many ways Christmas can lose its lustre.
In fact, it can easily become all-consuming and very stressful.

Should you shop early and methodically for gifts or
race around at the last minute to save time?

What on earth do you buy for the person who has everything?

Did you remember to send out all the cards and
order the turkey and ham? Yikes!

Meanwhile, no matter where you go, you can't escape
that accursed album of Christmas songs sung by the latest
tone-deaf sixteen-year-old pop sensation.

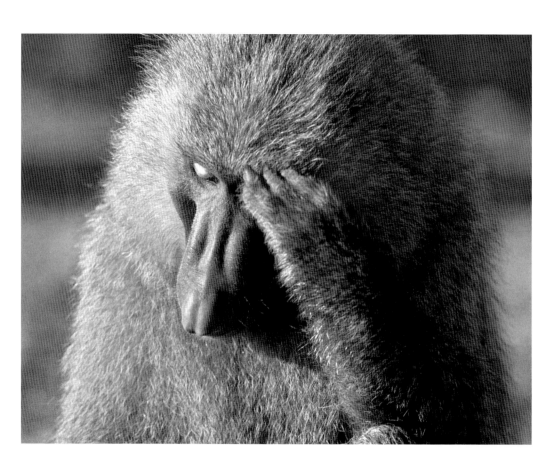

Soon you have a headache that feels as if a hot thumbtack
has been slowly pressed into the back of your left eyeball,
but you've got to keep going.

Dash off to buy a Christmas tree,

quickly zip out and get wrapping paper and ribbon
before the best designs vanish,

screech over to the supermarket to stock up the larder, and then do another thirteen hot laps of the local shopping centre in case you forgot somebody. It wouldn't be so bad if you got frequent-flier miles for your feet.

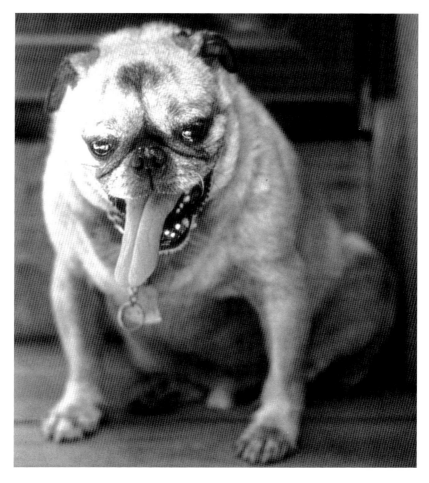

Soon you're worn down and utterly exhausted, but you still
haven't finished the first page of your ten-page list. You're starting to
lose both your Christmas spirit and your will to live,

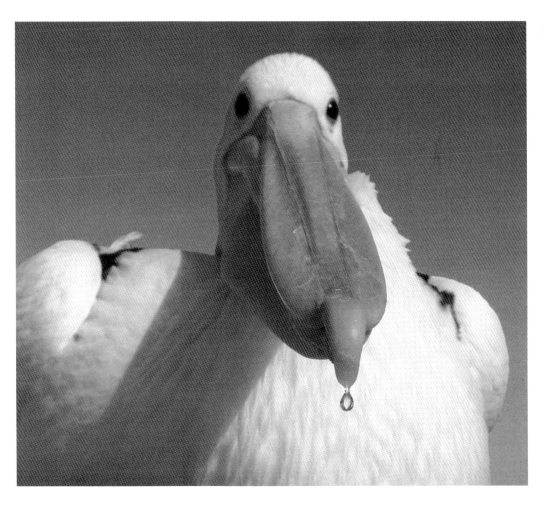

and now you feel a cold coming on.

Soon, too soon, the guests arrive. Quick, break out the fake smiles.
Time to exchange awkward kisses with thin-lipped relatives

and grit your teeth while normally absent uncles indulge in
rough-and-tumble with the smaller children under the bizarre illusion
that the poor little sprogs enjoy it.

Meanwhile, great-aunts and grandparents laugh so loudly and violently at their own feeble jokes they are in genuine danger of coughing up a kidney.

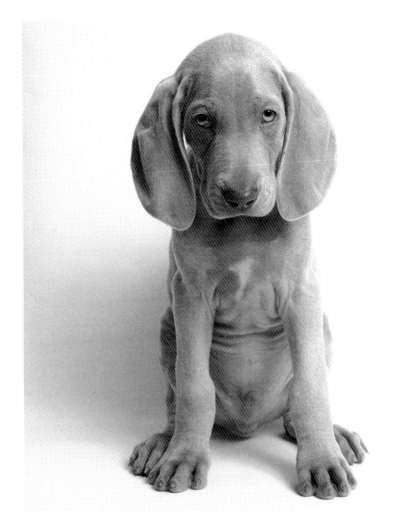

Then, the reaction to your carefully chosen gift is underwhelming.

"What do you mean, 'Batteries *not* included'?!"

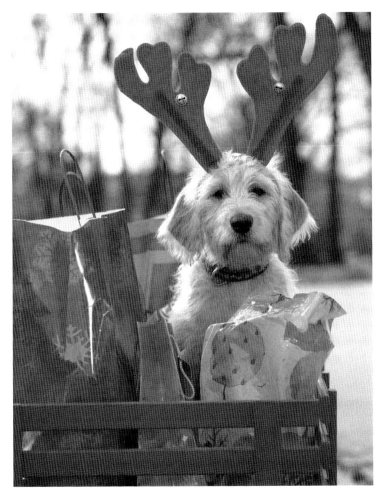

Most people think that Christmas has become perversely overcommercialized, and it's hard to disagree.

It has become painfully expensive, too. Every step at the local mall bites deeper and deeper into your hard-earned savings. In Ireland, the average Christmas expenditure per person is now almost €5,000!

Whatever seems to be the latest and greatest—*we must have it!*
Children drive their parents mad demanding kittens they won't feed, games
they won't play, and dirt bikes they won't ride for more than a month.

And off we go, like a legion of credit-card-wielding zombies,

marching off happily to be chewed up and spat out by
a giant faceless monster of soulless consumerism.

I strongly suspect that the reason super-intelligent, peace-loving beings from other galaxies have not made contact with us is because they have watched two old ladies choking each other over the last set of designer tea towels featuring seasonal motifs.

And God only knows what they think about the
gladiatorial spectacle of the January sales.

Nevertheless, malignant commercialization is merely a symptom.
The actual problem is that somehow, over time, the meaning of Christmas
has gotten all mixed up. The things that should be most important
no longer are. It's all back to front.

If Christmas has started to smell bad to you, don't blame others
for pooh-poohing the babe in a manger. Ask yourself, "Is it me?"

"Good heavens. It *is* me!"
Just like bad body odour, the source of most ills
is usually closer to home than you might want to believe.

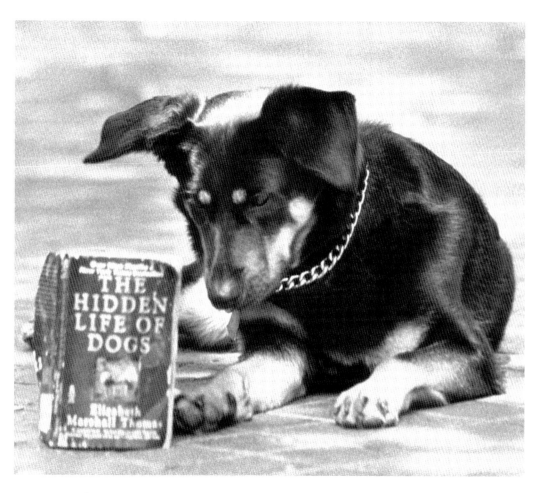

Examine your own motivations and behaviour, and be honest about your part in all of this. To some degree, we have brought this situation upon ourselves by buying into it.

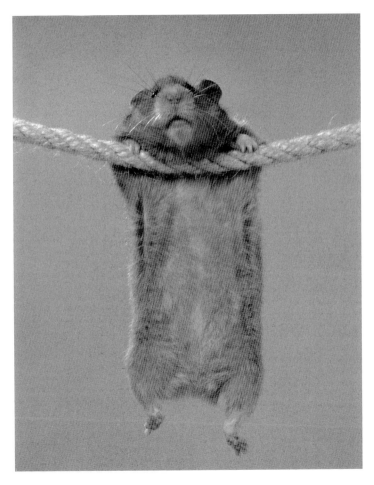

It's worth making some changes so that we can enjoy ourselves even more—after all, the Christmas season was not supposed to be merely endured.

These wonder-filled days and sacred hours were meant be treasured.
Always.

Rigorous clinical tests show there is no inherent magic power
in mistletoe or holly berries—only in our hearts.

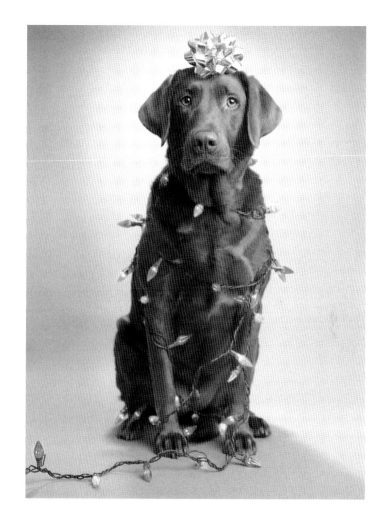

So instead of knocking yourself out to deck the halls,

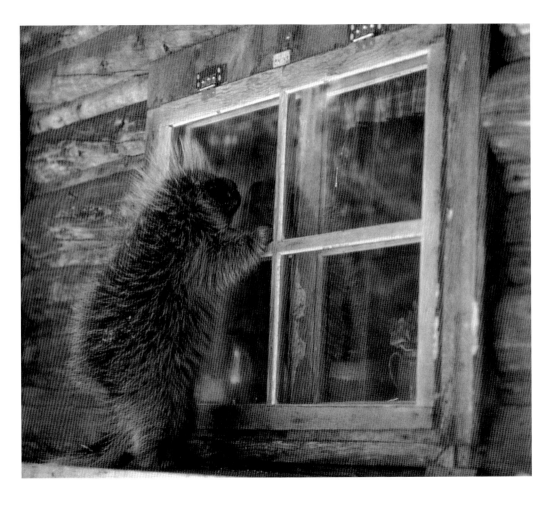

just let the spirit of Christmas come into your home—it's that simple.

And if you'd like some more free advice
about how to have a wonderful Christmas, here it is:

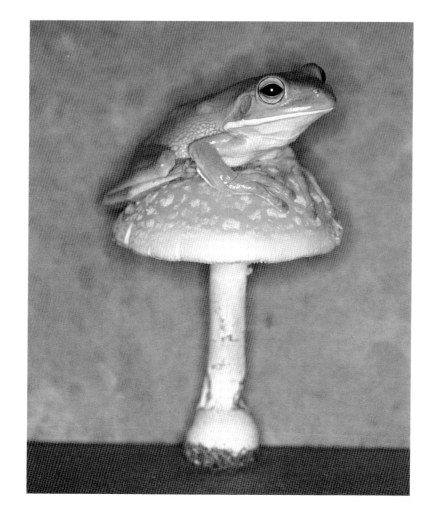

Be the star at the top of your tree.

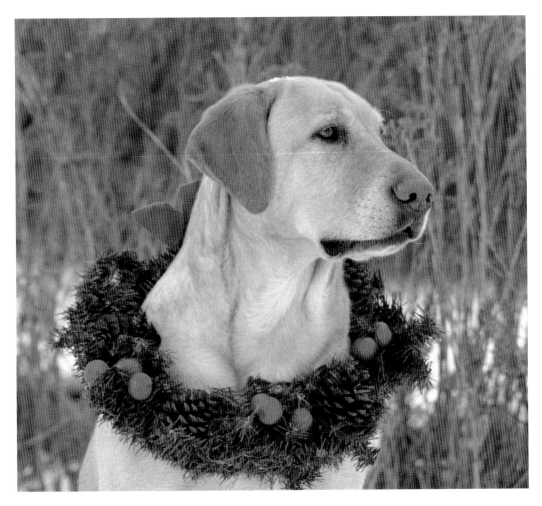

By which I mean, become a Christmas ambassador
and take the spirit with you wherever you go.

Imagine how you might react if the Creator, looking down upon us,
decided to send us an angel as a celestial messenger of Christmas
to grant us all one special wish.

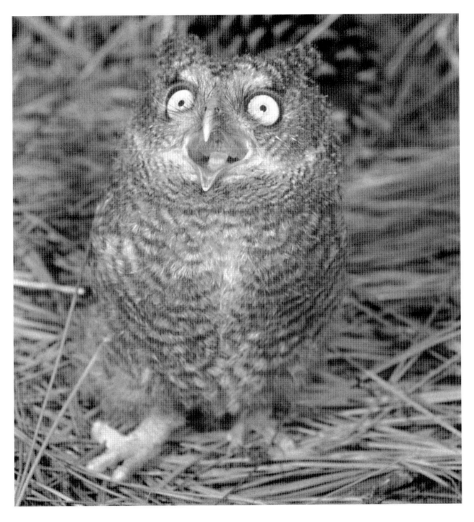

Obviously you'd be entitled to freak out a little bit,

but when you had recovered from the shock, what question would you ask, what one wish would you want granted by this beautiful, pure manifestation of peace, hope, and love? Well, I can certainly tell you what I *wouldn't* be asking . . .

"I wanna new cell phone, some diamond earrings, some new Nikes, and a mountain bike, and a 42-inch plasma TV, and a Harrods charge card . . . and hey, how about some of Nigella's sexy nesting bowls!"

Obviously we'd all be a lot happier if we spent less time
whining about what we wanted and more time being thankful
for the many good things we already enjoy.

There are very few things in life worth wishing for
beyond the health and happiness of our family and friends.
If you have that, you have it all.

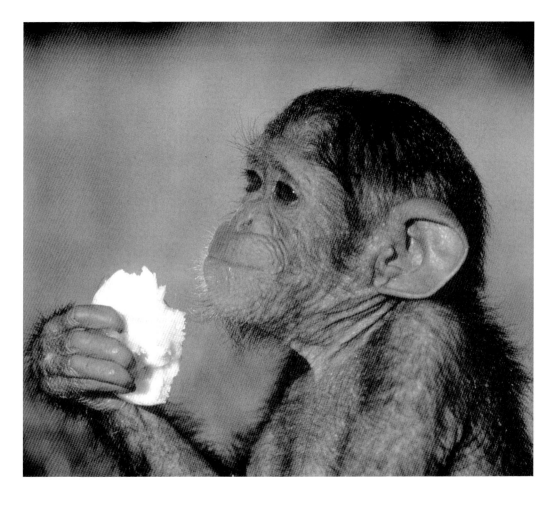

We should be grateful that we have enough to eat—let alone have the opportunity to indulge in delicious Christmas dinners.

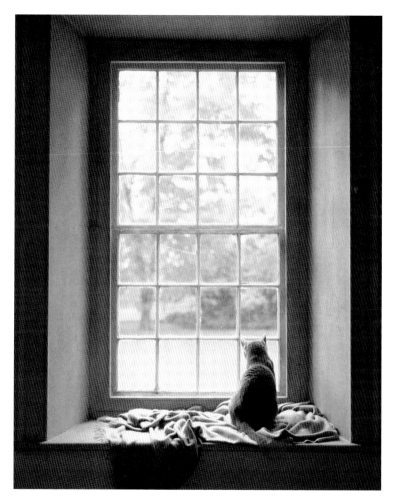

We should be grateful that we are not alone in this world and that, especially at Christmastime, we are surrounded by those we love.

One thing to keep in mind is that Christmas Day is celebrated
at many different times from September to February, depending on various
customs and beliefs. In other words, an "ordinary day" *becomes* Christmas Day
by virtue of the meaning we give it, not because of any ironclad rule.
Therefore, why can't every day be Christmas?

Okay, not literally, or we'd all need weekly liver transplants.

But why not vest every day with at least some of the values
and highlights that make Christmas so much more exciting and uplifting
than the other 364 days of the year?

Remember, every day gives you a fresh start, so it doesn't really matter so much what happened the year, month, or day before. You can make things right today, and that's what counts.

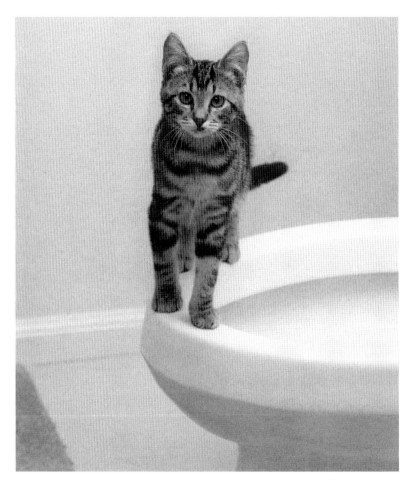

There is often a fine line between a great day and a lousy day, Christmas or otherwise. A little luck certainly helps, but preparation and imagination always make the biggest difference.

You don't have to reinvent the wheel—just add a little pizzazz to your routine.
Wear that outfit you thought was too wild for the office,

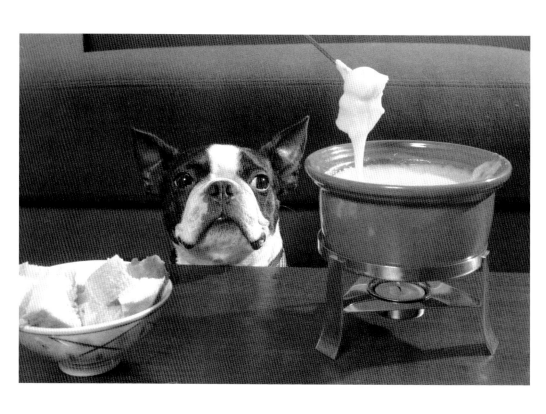

and, unless your medical alert bracelet warns you otherwise,
84   why not try something for lunch or dinner that you wouldn't normally eat?

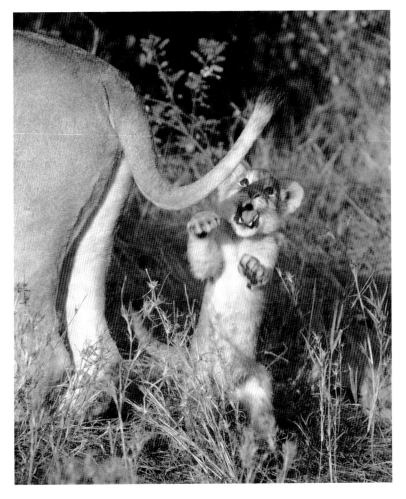

With a little bit of creative effort and a sense of humour, you'll soon realize
that all manner of Christmas delights are available every day.

The next step is to pass this on to your family,
your friends, and your colleagues.

Not only is this the true spirit of Christmas at its best but,
with the exception of chicken-pox, just about everything is more enjoyable
when you have someone to share it with.

At the end of the day we are all in this together.

So on this or any day, why not at least try to stop
making life hard for each other?

Share the love, baby!

If people abuse you, shrug it off and stun them with genuine good wishes.
They will feel worse, and you will feel better. It's a win-win!

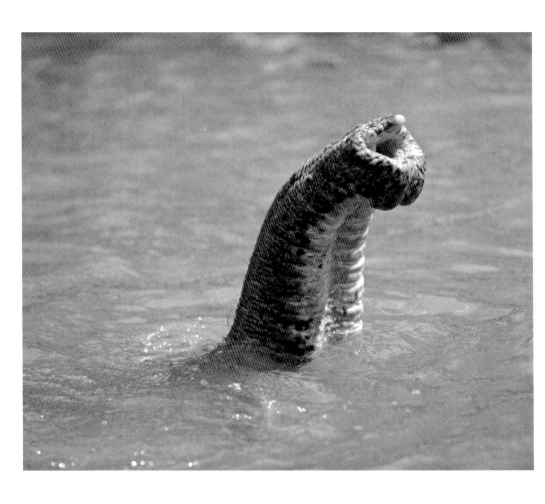

Christmas is all about making sacrifices—going miles out of your way
to touch the lives of others in the belief that you can make a difference.

And not just family and friends.

I also mean people you would never normally come in contact with.

To get the most out of Christmas, we just have to break through
the "me, me, me" barrier.

Put yourself in someone else's shoes for a while and think of what you could do to make them feel loved, appreciated, and joyful.

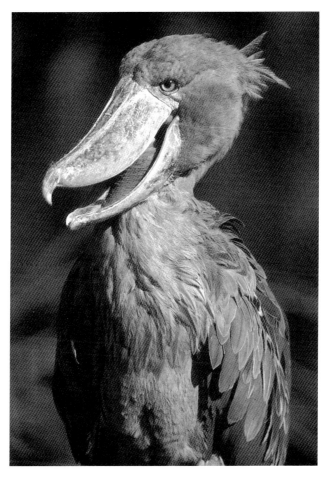

And hey, if it doesn't work out, you will then know all their weaknesses
in order to crush them once and for all, heh, heh, heh!
But I digress.

The first thing to remember is that none of this should cost a fortune.

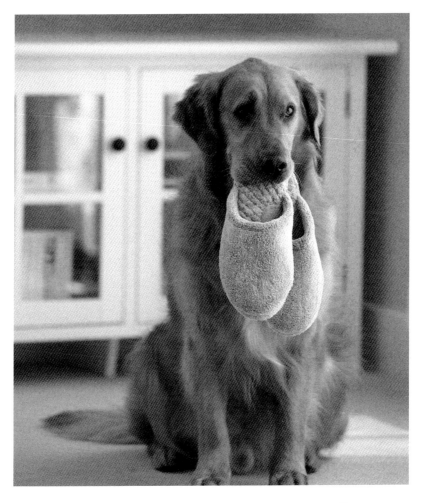

In fact, sometimes it costs nothing at all. Even the smallest gesture can mean an enormous amount.

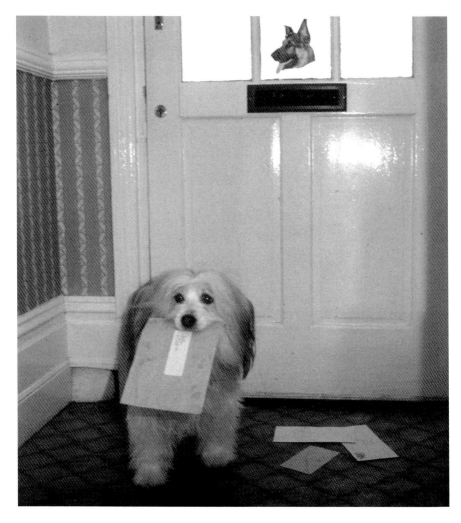

Who has not been moved to tears of joy by a simple card,

an unexpected phone call,

or a warm hug?

The meaning of Christmas is to give of yourself—to open up the joy in your heart and share it generously. If you do this properly, then every day will feel like . . . well, like Christmas.

I'm not saying you'll run around screaming, "Joy to the World!" at the top of your lungs. That would only terrify the very old and the very young and cause small animals to scatter into the path of oncoming traffic.

If you can just tiptoe a little out of your way—not even a full extra mile,
just a few inches more each day—you will certainly have more fun
and so will everyone who crosses your path.

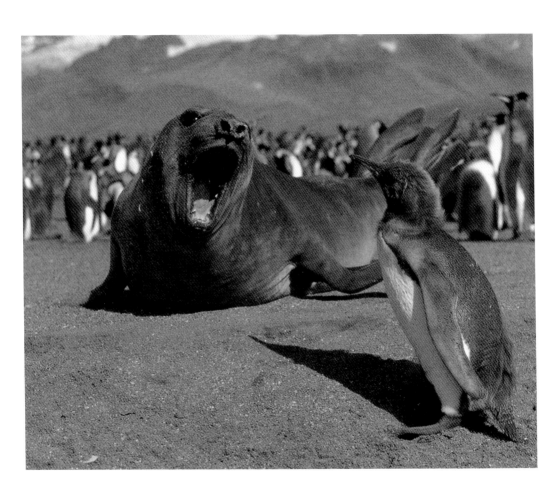

Then, when you greet them with a smile and say a cheery "Hello!"

you'll really be saying, "Merry Christmas!"

"Mewwy Cwithmath!"

"Me-rry Christ-mas!"

"MERRRRRY CHRISTMASSSSS!"

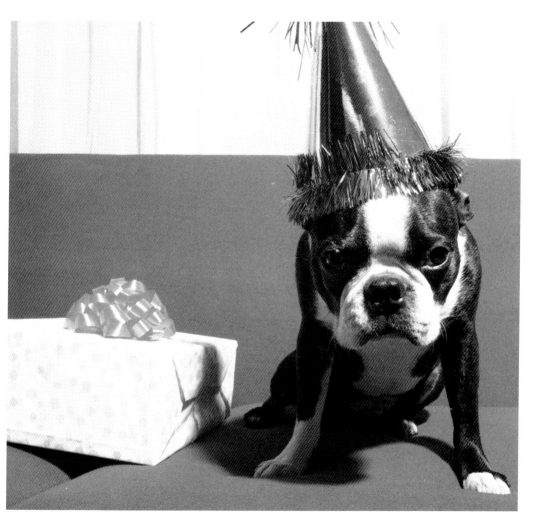

So don't just sit there. The best day of the year is about to begin.

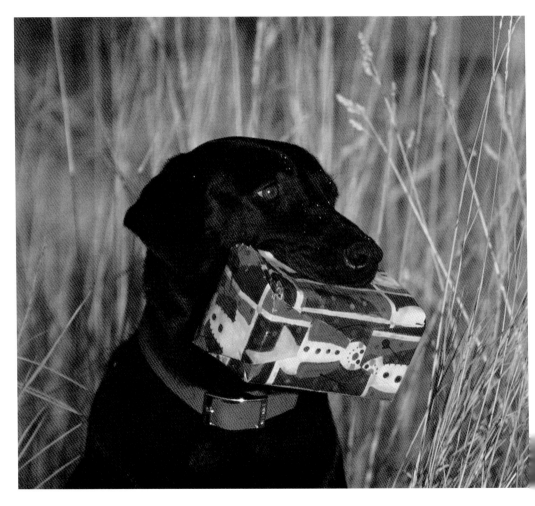

Pick it up and give it a shake—
you never know what good things might come out of it.

(P.S. Merry Christmas!)